EDITED BY

# EMILY TRUNKO

CREATOR OF THE POPULAR TUMBLR

*Dear My*
# BLANK

SECRET LETTERS
NEVER SENT

ILLUSTRATED BY LISA CONGDON

CROWN
NEW YORK

This book is dedicated to Rian,
as well as all the other followers and supporters
of Dear My Blank, and anyone else who's
written a letter they don't intend to send.

Text copyright © 2016 by Emily Trunko
Cover art and interior illustrations copyright © 2016 by Lisa Congdon
All rights reserved. Published in the United States by Crown Books for
Young Readers, an imprint of Random House Children's Books,
a division of Penguin Random House LLC, New York.
The letters that appear herein were originally submitted to the
Tumblr "Dear My Blank."

A NOTE ON FORMAT: While we fixed misspellings,
we have kept the unique text formatting of each
individual letter for authenticity.

Crown and the colophon are registered trademarks of
Penguin Random House LLC.
Visit us on the Web! randomhouseteens.com
Educators and librarians, for a variety of teaching tools,
visit us at RHTeachersLibrarians.com
Library of Congress Cataloging-in-Publication Data is available upon request.
ISBN 978-0-399-55742-2 (trade) — ISBN 978-0-399-55744-6 (ebook)
Printed in the United States of America
10 9 8 7 6 5 4 3 2 1
First Edition
Random House Children's Books supports the First Amendment
and celebrates the right to read.

# INTRODUCTION

Have you ever written a letter to someone without intending to send it?

If so, you're not alone.

My name's Emily, I'm fifteen years old, and I started a Tumblr called Dear My Blank in March 2015. It's a Tumblog containing anonymous submissions of unsent letters. When I started it, I wasn't expecting much. It was just a small idea fueled by the fact that I had a three-subject notebook full of unsent letters to crushes, friends, family, people I didn't speak to anymore, and anyone else who'd had an impact on my life, as well as a folder on my computer of the letters I'd written after filling up that notebook. The letters were important to me because they helped me get out emotions I wasn't able to express any other way. When I started the Tumblr, I was just curious about whether other people did the same thing as me.

But then, as thousands of people began sending in their letters, I realized that Dear My Blank was becoming much bigger than I'd ever expected. The media quickly caught on to the raw emotions expressed in the Dear My Blank submissions and helped to spread the word. My tiny Tumblr was thrust into the spotlight overnight, and the resulting submissions were amazing. People were using it to say things they'd never said before, to express feelings they'd tried to bury, to confess their crushes, and to get closure over the ends of relationships or after the death of someone important to them. What had started as a small project had quickly morphed into something that contained an incredible amount of human emotions, a cyber melting pot of sorrow and heartbreak and hope and new love. There were letters to family members, crushes, exes, friends, teachers, celebrities, and many more kinds of social connections.

Along with all the people getting closure by submitting their letters, I got something amazing from Dear My Blank as well—I met my boyfriend through it. We began talking several days after I started my Tumblr, when he submitted his own letter and I kept in contact with him. That's only one example of the relationships that have begun because of Dear My Blank. Another boy submitted a letter and his crush found it, realized he'd submitted it, and ended up contacting him. They were able to reveal their feelings to each other. Just like Rian and me, they're still together.

When a letter was sent in from someone asking what to do about controlling parents, the inbox was flooded with letters offering support and advice, numbers of hotlines, and sage words from personal experience. In the beginning of this introduction, I summarized Dear My Blank by calling it a blog. But it's become a lot more than just a blog. It's become a supportive community.

Dear My Blank has changed my life in so many ways. It was started nine months ago, and there are currently over thirty thousand submissions, with more arriving every day. I find it incredible that so many people trust me with their unsent letters. I feel so honored to be their keeper, and I plan to collect them for the rest of my life.

Emily Trunko
January 2016

Visit
dearmyblank.tumblr.com

Dear 17-year-old self,

You are beautiful. Remember that. Soon, all too soon, there will be people who tell you otherwise. So, when all the spectators have gone home, find a mirror. Look at all the parts of you that you hide beneath layers of self hate. Find the beauty in the fat, in the freckles, in the discolorations, in the acne, in the scars, in all the things that make you cringe. It will make the bullying easier to handle.

He will always be JUST your friend. It will hurt. Sometimes you will hang up the phone, only to cry yourself to sleep. But he is your friend, and he doesn't mean to hurt you. Once you leave for college, the 600 miles will seem like an ocean to yell across. So enjoy the pleasantly painful knots that he ties in your chest with each brush of his hand against yours.

Buy Mom flowers for no reason. Tell her every day how much you love her. When her kidneys fail, do not leave her side. It will all be over soon. And you will always regret not being there for every second you could.

E

DEAR YOUNGER ME,

that is not love.

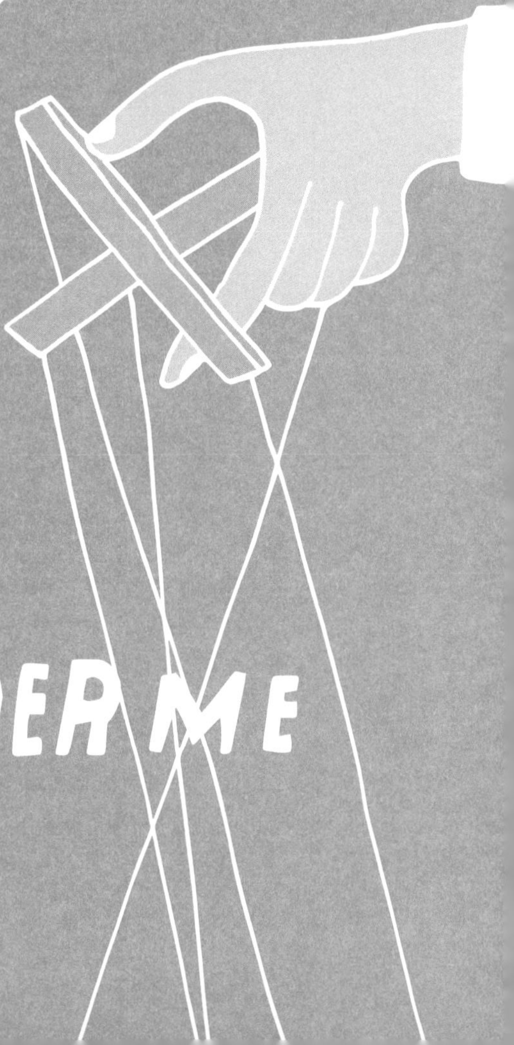

-OLDER ME

Past Self—

It will ruin the
friendship. He'll
hate you. It's not
worth it.

M

dear thirteen-year-old self,

1. he doesn't love you (and that's okay).
2. the braces will be worth it one day.
3. math doesn't get any easier. however, life is more than numbers. when you look at the sky, try not to count. trace constellations instead.
4. you're never too old to sing along to the *high school musical* soundtrack.
5. part your hair on the side from now on. it frames your face better.
6. you're not as mature as you think you are. give yourself space to grow.
7. your mother is the strongest woman you will ever meet. she will recover. hair grows back. her own body hasn't given up on her. you shouldn't either.
8. always wear sunscreen.
9. you're too young to think about college. there's plenty of time for that in the future.
10. keep writing.

love, mae

Dear my body,

You did nothing wrong. I don't hate you.
I just dislike the fact that I have to own a
body, to live in it. But that's not your
fault. I just don't know how to live in
you. I always feel that you're there, and
sometimes I wish you could disappear.
But that's not possible. I have to learn
how to be with you, to not feel like
you're a burden. It makes me sad when
people criticize you, because I know that
I love you, you are a part of me.

Sometimes I also hate when people say they find you pretty, because that reminds me that you're there.

Sometimes I feel like you're more important than me, and I feel like it's unfair, because I'm the important one. But you're important too. I owe you so much. I'm sorry to think such horrible things about you, I really am.

I hope we will be fine.

I love you.

Me.

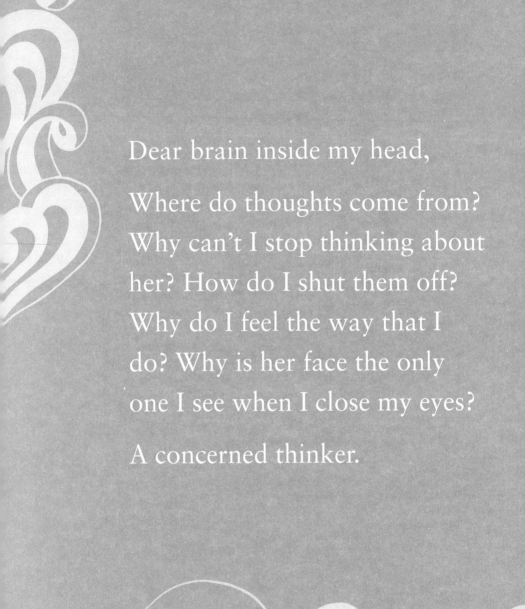

Dear brain inside my head,

Where do thoughts come from?
Why can't I stop thinking about
her? How do I shut them off?
Why do I feel the way that I
do? Why is her face the only
one I see when I close my eyes?

A concerned thinker.

DEAR 10-YEAR-OLD SELF,

IT'S NOT YOUR FAULT.

IT NEVER WAS AND

STILL ISN'T.

YOUR

17-YEAR-OLD

SELF

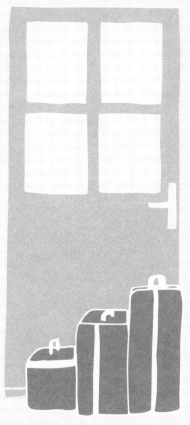

Dear 18-Year-Old Self,

Slow down—everything is going to be fine. You aren't going to fail at anything you care about or anything important. Be less afraid. Less afraid to talk to people. Less afraid to assert yourself. Less afraid that time alone is a bad thing. It's okay that you cry a few times a week. Living away from home is hard, and that part won't get easier. You will cry less. Walk away from the things that take more than they give. Give to the things that nourish you or make you happy. Give more of yourself to less things.

At 21, you are going to realize that you don't need to count the moments where you are happy. You will be happy almost all the time. Movies about injustices are going to make you cry. Don't stop watching them. They are going to give you purpose. Don't freak out that you change your life goal with every movie. As long as you plan to do good, you are staying true to yourself. Stop comparing yourself to those around you. Their struggles do not invalidate your own. Their successes do not diminish yours. You will never have all the answers. You will always have some. Taking your life a day at a time is not a failure—you are not a failure.

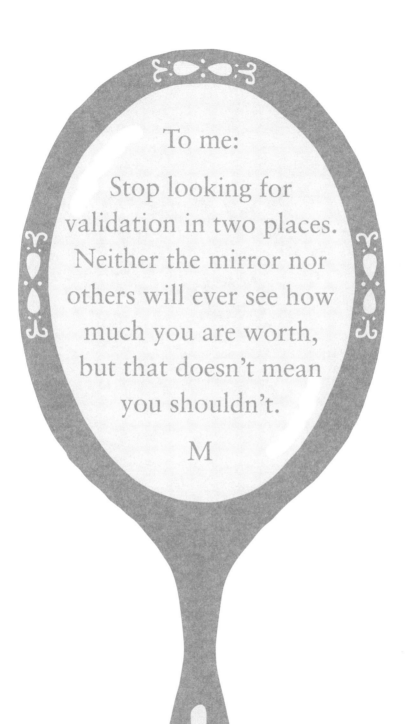

To me:

Stop looking for validation in two places. Neither the mirror nor others will ever see how much you are worth, but that doesn't mean you shouldn't.

M

DEAR 18-YEAR-OLD SELF,

EVERYTHING HAS WORKED OUT SO FAR. JUST KEEP GOING. AND MAYBE RETHINK THE FRENCH CLASSES.

-ME

to whoever will listen.

i've been thinking about black holes a lot.
how their gravity is so strong it bends time
and space. how you'd be stretched down
to atoms passing the event horizon.

i kind of feel like i'm being stretched out to atoms.
like i'm falling apart and becoming so metaphorically
thin that i'm transparent. but, as nothing that happens
past the event horizon affects the universe outside of it,
nothing that i'm feeling is affecting anyone in the
outside world either.

the event horizon is a point of no return.
nothing, not even light, can escape it.

i wonder what will happen when i pass the event
horizon and fully submerge myself into the black hole.

there are theories that if you enter a black hole
under a specific angle, you'll survive and hit the
bottom of it. the chances are incredibly small.

i doubt i'll survive.

DEAR WORLD,

I'M NOT QUIET BECAUSE I'M SHY.
I'M QUIET BECAUSE EVERY WAKING
MINUTE THERE ARE THOUSANDS OF
THOUGHTS SWIRLING AROUND IN MY
HEAD. AND I'M CONSTANTLY SORTING
THROUGH THEM, REMEMBERING THE
GOOD ONES AND FIGHTING THE BAD
ONES. I'M AN OVERTHINKER. IT'S
WHO I AM. PLEASE JUST BE PATIENT
WITH ME. I SWEAR I WANT TO
TALK TO YOU. I JUST NEED SOME
EXTRA TIME TO GET MY THOUGHTS
IN ORDER.

LOVE,
ME

Dear anyone with dyslexia,

You have a lot to give to the world. You think differently.
You think creatively. Maybe you can't read very well, or
spell very well—or whatever your dyslexia makes you
struggle with (I know how many things can get affected
by dyslexia)—but that doesn't mean you can't do great,
wonderful things. You are not dumb or stupid or anything
else negative due to your dyslexia. You are creative, clever,
and wonderful. Don't let anyone let you forget that.
Yes, being dyslexic makes life harder to cope with at times.
And on bad days it can make you want to scream with
anger. I'm not going to say you aren't different, because
you are, but remember that it's not in a negative way.
And if you ever feel down, look at all the names of famous
dyslexics. They are the ones who changed the world.
And you could be added to that list one day. Keep your
chin up, even on the hardest days, even if that seems like
the most impossible thing to achieve.

Love from,
A fellow dyslexic who knows your pain and can also easily
forget these things a lot of times herself, but hopes maybe
if you remember any of this just once it can help you in
some way on one of those awful days where you just need
an extra push of strength because it seems like you are
climbing a mountain to do the simplest of tasks

Dear lgbt+ people,

You are loved, you are loved,
you are loved.

Please, don't let the hatred of this
world of ours convince you that you
are not worthy or deserving of love.

Don't let them dismiss your
identities.

There's nothing more to say.
You are loved. You are important.
You are worthy.

—D

Dear Brave People,

I realise that it appears I'm fearless. I can make that
presentation with ease, I can stand near the edge of the
cliff and look down, and I can befriend that spider in the
bathroom. (He's called Steve.)

But recently I've realised that's not what makes people
brave. *Brave* has a different meaning.

I'm afraid of people leaving. After I watched my
best friend become someone else's and I was forced into
befriending my childhood bully, I realised I don't want to let
myself go through this again. I see my fear come through
when questioning my boyfriend's affections. I see it when
I distance myself from my friends who are going to leave
for university. I see it in my overanalysis of my parents'
relationship and paranoia over a possible divorce.

I don't want to be alone.

I'm afraid of failure. I aced my exams and the bar has
moved up again. I have those high expectations along with
everyone else, but I know now that maybe the tower is just
too tall, and I should've built stronger foundations. I act like
I know what I'm doing, but really I'm drifting away from the
shore faster and faster.

I don't want to let anyone down.

I'm afraid of change. I don't know where I lie anymore.

I thought I knew what to do in my future, but I can't bear to think that I'm now not so sure. I thought I was completely straight, but now it's internal agony as I'm not so sure. Turns out I thought a lot of things.

I don't want my life to not be the way I expected.

I may not be scared of crowds. Or the dark. Or small spaces. *But I am afraid.*

I am afraid of responsibility; I am afraid of not living up to expectations, of the changing future, of growing up, not knowing, sex, relationships, hardship, secrets, grades, judgment, falling short, loneliness, change, confusion, arguments, curiosity, love, hate, losing, pressure, differences, honesty, lies.

I am afraid of *me*.

Yet, despite this, I know I am brave. I know I am brave because I've accepted my invisible fears and haven't let them overcome me.

I want you to know that you're brave because you know your fears. You're brave because you introduced yourself. You're brave because you said "No, I don't understand." You're brave because you're here.

I hope you can learn from me and be brave in your own way. I know I am.

—B

Dear whoever is reading this,

I wish I could find a way to take all of your
sadness away and replace it with happiness.
I can't. But I can try. You are worth it. You have
entire galaxies within you and an entire life
ahead of you. You will do so much and meet
so many more people. Keep going. Things will
get hard. But they will also get better. Keep
smiling. It's okay to cry every once in a while.
It's okay to spend time alone. But it's important
to keep going. Good luck.

Love,
A

Dear you,

Yes, you. The person reading this right now.

If you're anything like me, sometimes you might feel like you don't matter. Like you're completely ordinary, unremarkable, boring, invisible. Like if you disappeared, nobody would notice.

Don't. Don't feel that way.

You are extraordinary. You are remarkable. You are interesting. You are dazzling. Your presence is noticed and appreciated. You are moonbeams and starlight, a sugar rush, the sound of laughter like bells. You are a soft breeze on a sweltering summer day, the wonder of a year's first snow, and the magic of a million smiling faces.

You mean something to someone out there. You mean something to someone right here. You are important, and the footprints you leave in this world make a difference. Even though you might not always realize it, you are wonderful.

You matter. And I am happy you exist.

reader,

How to describe my parents in three words:

## controlling and abusive

(but not physically anymore)

I need help. I need to leave. But I have nowhere to go. Please, if anybody can do something or give me advice, I don't have much time.

They've had me lie to family, my friends, neighbors, and the school counselors about my life.

I've kept my life behind doors a secret for nine years, and it has gotten bad. But I can't go to authority or a social worker. I have siblings who are in a different situation than me.

I'm afraid to reach out to my parents, and I can't explain why. But I have voice recordings of all the times I've tried. The recordings are worse than any violent movie scene.

Somebody please write back.

—s

Dear young mothers-to-be,

I know it's terrifying to think in a few months' time you'll be a mother, you'll be responsible for this tiny human who will count on you for everything.

I know there will be people who say you're never gonna cope. You'll feel useless and feel like you're a bad mother. You may even feel like giving up.

Please don't give up. Hold your head up high and do your damned hardest to prove everyone who doubts you wrong. You can do it. Being a mother isn't easy at all, especially as a young mother because we get ridiculed all the time. It doesn't matter if you're 15 or 35. Age doesn't define you as a mother. Only you can do that.

From one young mother to another,
X

Dear Someone,

Whoever you are, whoever the fates had possibly decided to pair me up with for my end-all of loves, I'm so sorry.

I wish I could promise that we'd meet someday, that we'd love someday, but I can't. I really want to, though.

I want to take naps with you, and watch movies with you, and annoy you with how slowly I grocery shop because I can't decide on what brand of detergent is better. I want you to run your hands through my hair and scratch my back when I'm lazy. I want to smile at you awkwardly when my mother inevitably embarrasses me at dinner.

I want to apologize for making a weird dying groaning sound in my sleep. I want to apologize for being a couple degrees warmer than the average person. I want to argue over something stupid (but actually very important) like superhero characters and powers. I want to pretend to be annoyed by your morning breath or stinky feet. I want to draw you (maybe sometimes on you) when you sleep. I want to write stories about us. I want to share songs I heard and liked with you. I want to share a bag of chips with you.

I want to get food poisoning with you. I want to baby you (or tolerate your need to be babied) when you catch a cold. I want to rub your stomach when you get indigestion. I want to see your look of exasperation when I trip and hurt myself because sometimes I'm the clumsiest person you'll ever meet. I want you to deal with my crybaby self because I will always cry when a sad scene shows up in a movie. (Guess who's crying right now?)

I want to hear you tell me I don't need makeup, even if you're just saying it because I'm taking too long to get ready. I want to hear it even if I won't believe it. I want to hear it even though I'll reply that it doesn't matter because I wear makeup for me. I want to show you who I am at my worst, the kind of person I'm afraid to show other people. I want you to do the same. I want to have trust and love and faith in each other.

I want to apologize to you for always telling people that I don't believe in relationships. I want to apologize for pretending to be unaffected by this. I want to apologize even though I'll never be able to say it to your face. I want so much.

I want to not have to write this letter because I'm dying and I'll probably never meet you, or just reject you even if I did. I'm sorry if I already met you and pushed you away.

More than anything, I want you to be happy, so much happier than I could have ever tried to make you.

I'm sorry we'll never have this, but I don't really have much longer. I'm just so sorry.

I would have given you the world.

Regretfully,
A Love Lost

For the broken hearts,

I promise it gets better.

    I promise that the minutes and hours will go by faster and that the ache in your chest will stop.

    I promise that the day you can forgive and realize that you don't have to feel this way will come.

    I promise you that right now, no matter what age you are, it will hurt. But pain is temporary.

    I promise that months or even years from now you'll look back and realize how silly you're acting. Although it doesn't feel silly.

    I promise that your relationship with them may or may not bloom into at least a friendship.

    I promise it'll stop hurting. Give it time, give yourself time to be an individual again. Find the confidence to do things on your own. Reconnect with the friends you pushed away. Form a better self. Be selfish. Stop thinking about their opinion.

xoxoxo,

M

R,

You ask me a lot if I still love you the way I did in the beginning. Sometimes I say yes, but I think the answer is no. I don't love you the way I did in the beginning. I love you much more. Our love has grown and changed, but in the best ways possible.

I'll always love you, even if you break my heart.

E

J,

YOU once told me that if I can see the sun, then I am standing within its radiance. That's how I feel whenever I see you ... as though I am standing within your rays, which encompass me and are inescapable.

— S

KEVIN,

I WASN'T ALL tHAt COLD. I stOLE YOUR SWEAtSHIRt BECAUSE It SMELLS LIKE YOU. I WISH YOU HAD LEt ME KEEP It.

-H

J,

I am torn between telling you
everything, and telling you
nothing.

   Maybe silence is safer than
letting you in. But my heart
is clawing its way out of my
mouth and

I LOVE YOU

I LOVE YOU

I LOVE YOU

I LOVE YOU

There, I said it.

T

Oppa,

I love you dearly and always.
I swear you have the universe in your
fingertips because every time you trace
them down my jaw I can feel
planets forming and breaking
apart in my stomach and stars being born
in my rib cage. I love you, my boy made of
universe dust. I am afraid of space and time
and everything in between, but you still
make me want to explore even the
darkest galaxies.

Thank you for that.
Kohai

Dear Earth,

Sometimes I think that love is the biggest lie ever told, humanity's hardest effort to convince itself that it's morally better than the savagery it's capable of.

Other times, I'm quite happy with my girlfriend.

—M

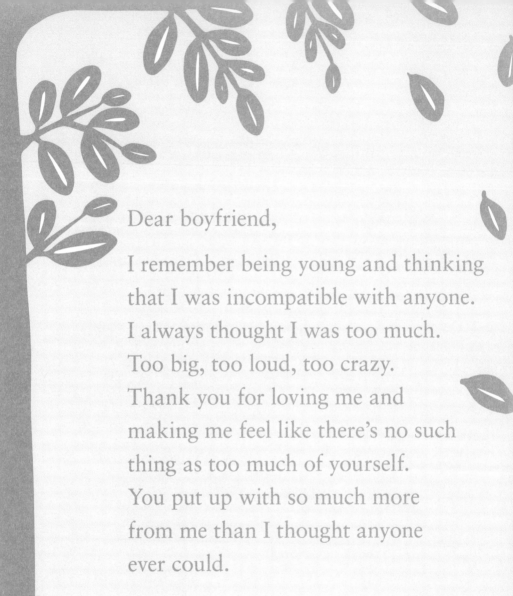

Dear boyfriend,

I remember being young and thinking
that I was incompatible with anyone.
I always thought I was too much.
Too big, too loud, too crazy.
Thank you for loving me and
making me feel like there's no such
thing as too much of yourself.
You put up with so much more
from me than I thought anyone
ever could.

Love,
Your girlfriend

m,
I love you
LIKE DEADPOOL LOVES
BATMAN. HE DOESN'T.
BUT EVEN IF HE DID,
THEY'RE FROM
COMPLETELY DIFFERENT
UNIVERSES.

- R

P,
i'm a prisoner
to my addictions.
and you are my
addiction.
                    - f

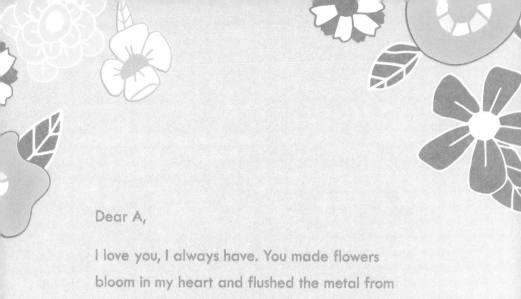

Dear A,

I love you, I always have. You made flowers
bloom in my heart and flushed the metal from
my veins. I've never told you, but I guess that's
because I knew you would hate me. I knew
how scared you were of letting people care
about you. I told you all of my secrets, my
confessions, my fears, and you were always
there to listen to me, to show me such a deep
level of understanding that I couldn't even begin
to comprehend. I love you, A. I always will, no
matter what happens in my life. You'll always
be my soulmate.

From,

S

B,

All I want to do is kiss you in the rain and dance on stage and talk about our favorite TV shows and stargaze and just breathe the same air as you for more than a few passing moments at a time.

All I want to hear is you saying the same things to me that I think of saying to you.

All I want to know is if any of this is worth it, if I'm making a good choice by choosing to love you.

Maybe I don't really have a say in what happens next, but I know that what I want is you.

C

T,

I LOVE THE WAY YOU
EXPLAIN WHY IT RAINS.
I REALLY DO THINK THE
SKIES ARE JUST SAD
BECAUSE OF HOW FAR
APART WE ARE. BUT WE'LL
SEE EACH OTHER SOON,
I PROMISE.

a

Dear K,

When I say you are **perfect**, I mean your mind and your spirit, not just your body.

When I say **I'll be there for you**, I mean every minute of every day for the rest of my life.

When I say **let me in**, I mean into your heart.

When I call you **my love**, I mean the love of my life.

When I say you are the **most beautiful** woman I have ever met, I mean in every sense, in every lifetime since the beginning of time.

When I say I am **jealous**, I mean of your coffee cup and your gloves because they can touch your lips and hold your hands.

When I say **I will come to you**, I mean just say the word, anytime, day or night, and I will be on the first plane.

When I say **I love you**, I don't mean just as a friend.

I don't want to just be your friend.

Love,

K

KEITH,
MY DISTANCE ISN'T
BECAUSE I DON'T
LOVE YOU. MY
DISTANCE IS
BECAUSE I'M AFRAID
THAT I DO.

C

A,

You healed all
my broken pieces.

Love,
N

J—

HOW CAN
BEING WITH
YOU FEEL SO
RIGHT, YET WE'RE
SO WRONG FOR
EACH OTHER?

WE'RE LIKE FIRE AND
GASOLINE. WE'RE BEAUTIFUL
AND WE BURN SO BRIGHT AND
HAVE SO MUCH WARMTH, YET
WE DESTROY EACH OTHER
UNTIL THERE'S NOTHING
LEFT. I MISS YOU EVERY DAY.
AND I WILL ALWAYS LOVE
YOU, BABY. —A

S,

I've fallen in love and
he's made me realize
that all the times we
said "I love you"
we were wrong.

—S

J,

I adore you, and all the moments I get to spend with you. But you're the ocean, and I'm just another beach bum who you've been kind enough to let swim in your waves. I think your tide has pulled me in, and the butterflies inside my stomach are flying away and I'm starting to realize how vulnerable I've left myself. How susceptible to you I really am. And I guess that's the funny thing about oceans. I'm enchanted by you, but just because I'm being swept off my feet doesn't mean I'm not drowning.

VM

A,

YOU'RE MY
11:11
WISH EVERY
TIME.
-Z

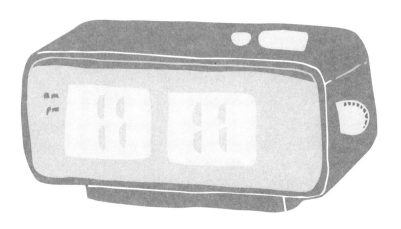

H,

They say that your first love
hurts the most. But I disagree. I think
second loves hurt much more. Second loves
are the ones to show you that love still exists.
After losing a first love, the world seems hopeless
and bleak; you're convinced you'll never love another
person "like that" ever again. But then second loves
waltz into your life and trace your scars with kisses.
A world you once considered dull brightens and
beautifies when they look into your eyes. Even after
being so hurt, even after losing your innocence, second
loves do the impossible: they make you believe in love
again. You hesitatingly open yourselves up to them.
You tell them your dreams and fears. You dare to hope
that love isn't a onetime thing after all.

So when you lose your second love, you start to
wonder if you missed your second chance.

I fell for you when I thought I'd never fall again.

T

# DOROTHEA,

i FiNiSHED WRITING MY OPERA. YOU'RE OFFiCiALLY MY MUSE; AND I'M STILL IN LOVE WiTH YOU. NOW ALL i HAVE tO DO is ASK YOU tO SiNG THE LEAD ROLE.

tHE ENDING'S GREAT— YOU'LL LOVE it.  _J

Daniel,
If sunshine had a
human form, it
**WOULD BE YOU.**
I am so PROUD
OF YOU.

YOURS truly,
DEB

Dear A & C,

I'm holding on so tight, I swear. But maybe that's the problem. You were going to be the bridesmaids at my wedding. We were going to visit each other in the future. We were always going to be best friends, and I don't care how naive that sounds because it gave me infinite hope to think that we'd always love each other.

And even though it kills me, maybe it's time for me to let go.

All my love, E

T,

I wish I hadn't deleted all your texts. I was hoping I could delete you, but honestly I think about you all the time. We haven't spoken in exactly a year; we haven't been friends for more than two. I still don't understand what happened.

R

Dear O (or L, you're both),

I'm so sorry we don't talk anymore.
We were the giggly ones in class and I
have only now learned the importance of
holding on to the friends you have, and I
know it wasn't just me, but I am definitely
more to blame. I was the one who stopped
writing, and I'm sorry.

 All I know is you are so kind
and have always been such a
positive person that your current
friends are very lucky. I genuinely wish you
all the best in your life.

T

dear d,

i'm so glad we're not friends anymore. i don't miss you at all and i feel like myself again.

from, j

A List of things a friend
should Never Do:

* **YOU SHOULD Not** take the day
  off to go shopping with your best
  friend's boyfriend.

* **You should Not** make her feel
  like a third wheel when she's with
  you and her boyfriend.

* **You should not** buy him a cupcake
  while she stands there and refuse
  to get her one after.

* **You should Not** flirt with her
  now-ex in front of her a week
  after he ended it.

* **You should Not** leave her on
  her own and not support her
  in a breakup for the boy instead.

* **You should Not** defend him when
  she is expressing her feelings on where
  they as a couple went wrong, which
  is none of your business.

* **You SHOULD Not** tell her you want to be her friend despite everything and then stop talking to her when she's making such an effort.

* **You SHOULD Not** consider liking him.

* **You SHOULD Not** lead him on so three weeks later he tells you he fell in love with you.

* **You SHOULD Not** get together less than three weeks after our 11-month relationship ended.

* **You SHOULD Not** expect her to stay.

Sorry for not realising this was your to-do list, MEGAN.

Dear best friend,

You recently fell in love with my friend, and I set you up and I am so extremely happy for you. But now I'm left alone, because you always go to him for comfort and for advice, for everything you used to come to me for. Why have you abandoned me? I miss the old best friend, not this new replacement.

—A

Dear Melissa,

I'm not sure why you picked a guy over so many friendships. Especially one that talks so badly about you behind your back. You deserve a better guy, but when you finally wake up, we won't be here. We deserve a better friend.

Leslie

L,

I know shit's hard right now.
I know you feel alone, and I
know you miss her like hell. But,
friend, I am never, ever giving up
on you. You mean so much to me.
If you don't think you can make
it through the night, I want you
to call me. I'll try my best to help
you through. I love you. You are
so important to everyone here.
I can't wait for the day that you
realize that.

M

DEAR M,
THANK YOU
FOR BEING MY ROCK,
AND FOR BEING THE
LIGHT AT THE END OF
THE TUNNEL.
I CAN'T WAIT TO
SEE YOU AGAIN.
YOU'RE MY BEST
FRIEND. S

Dear E,

We've been best friends since we were four and you pushed me off the Batman bike in nursery. We're always together and we tell each other everything. You were the first person I came out to and you took me in when my parents found out. You've trusted me with so many of your secrets and I am honoured, but there's something that I've been keeping from you.

Your brother is a year older than you, and I know you think the world of him. He feels the same way about you. We've been dating for over a year now; we've been keeping it from you because neither of us wanted to hurt you. I love him, E. I'm completely and utterly, heart-hammering-in-my-chest-every-time-I-even-hear-his-name in love with him, and it kills me that I've been keeping this from you.

You know I've been in a secret relationship, and you were pissed that I wouldn't tell you who it was. I know this is the coward's way of telling you, but you tell me how much you love this blog, so I thought I could tell you on here because we both know I'm no good at face to face.

I love you so much, E, and we've been through so much together and I am truly honoured that you're still in my life, you and your son, who you know I adore to death. I just hope you don't hate me, or your brother, for keeping this from you.

I hope this isn't goodbye.

Love,

A

Aaron (the A who wrote to E, confessing your love),

I read your letter and it made me cry. Why you and my brother felt the need to hide your love is beyond me! And I know you would never have said it to my face because yeah, you're no good with face to face, so I'm sending you this letter so maybe it's not as awkward for you when we see each other next.

You've been avoiding me for the past few days and now I know why. I always thought you and my brother would make a cute couple, but I guess you already do! You deserve happiness after all you've been through, and supporting me through everything, you truly deserve to be happy. I hope Liam gives you that.

I'm upset that you both felt that you couldn't tell me, but if you and Liam are happy, that's all I care about.

I hope you see this before I come round. You're not going to get rid of me that easily!

Make sure he looks after you.

Your best friend who would
still push you off the Batman bike,
Emily

C,

YOU WERE ONCE MY BEST FRIEND. I DON'T HATE YOU. I'M NOT MAD AT YOU.

I MISS YOU.

I WISH I WAS BRAVE ENOUGH TO TEXT YOU AGAIN.

—A

Dear Madeline,

I miss you. I never got to meet you. I never heard your voice and I never saw your smile. Though I imagine it's a lot like mine. And yet I miss you so much.

Every time I see another set of twins just like us, I miss you even more. Seeing other twins, seeing the life I could have had with you, just rips another hole through my heart. I never met you, but I still feel the hole where you're supposed to be. It's unfair. It's too hard. And it's so many things it shouldn't be.

I should be sharing a room with you. I should be telling you all the things I can't tell anyone. But it's not like that. One day we'll be together again, but until then you have left a hole in me that cannot be filled by anyone else. And I'm left missing you.

All the love in the world
from your other half,
K

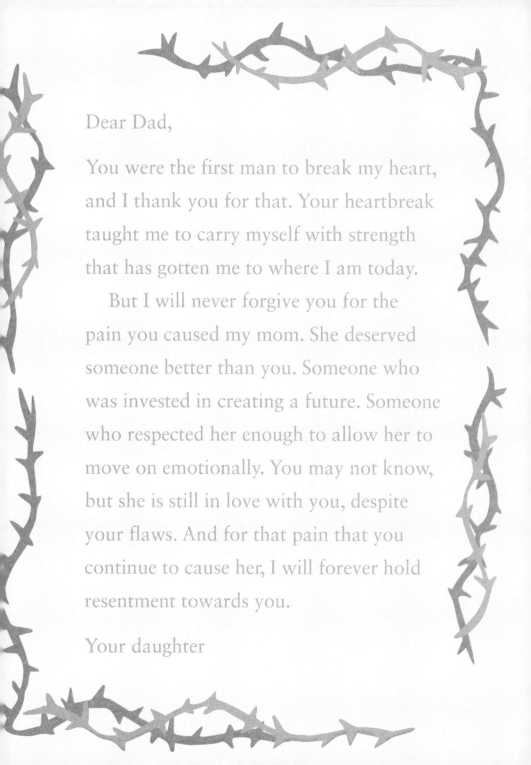

Dear Dad,

You were the first man to break my heart, and I thank you for that. Your heartbreak taught me to carry myself with strength that has gotten me to where I am today.

But I will never forgive you for the pain you caused my mom. She deserved someone better than you. Someone who was invested in creating a future. Someone who respected her enough to allow her to move on emotionally. You may not know, but she is still in love with you, despite your flaws. And for that pain that you continue to cause her, I will forever hold resentment towards you.

Your daughter

DEAR MOM, I'M BI. I WISH YOU COULD ACCEPT THAT. I'M SO TIRED OF HIDING. – YOUR DAUGHTER

Dear Dad,

I'm terrified that you won't get to walk me
down the aisle at my wedding. Considering
I don't dream of marriage the way that
some people do, I'm even more terrified
that you won't live to see my dreams come
true. You have been a part of every major
event in my life from my first breath
to moving into my first college dorm.
And it scares me that this could come to an
end. Please don't leave me.

Love you with all my heart even
when I think I hate you,
Your daughter

Mom,

You have always given me the necessities
to survive, but I am lacking your attention.
I am an only child; I do not have built-in best
friends. You are a single mom; I do not have
another adult to guide me when you're
busy. You give me attention for
poor grades and bad choices, but
I need you to be around to share fun
moments. I need you to come home on Friday
and Saturday nights. I need you to tell me that I
have a curfew. I am older now, but I need you to
pick a date night with me over a date night with
your boyfriend. Don't get me wrong, I think you are
wonderful, but I don't want to be a nuisance. I just
want to be with you, to look up to you, and to learn
from you.

Love,
A daughter who needs you

Dear my son,

The things that frustrate me
about you are the same things
I struggle with myself every day.
(I wish that meant I had the
answers.) I love you so much
and I am proud of you,
even when I yell.
I know you'll be amazing.

Xo,
Mom

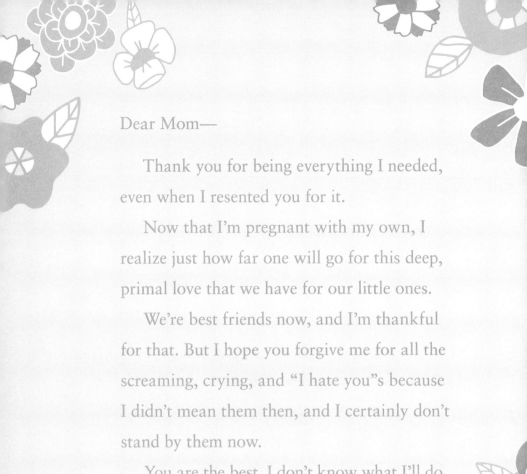

Dear Mom—

Thank you for being everything I needed,
even when I resented you for it.

Now that I'm pregnant with my own, I
realize just how far one will go for this deep,
primal love that we have for our little ones.

We're best friends now, and I'm thankful
for that. But I hope you forgive me for all the
screaming, crying, and "I hate you"s because
I didn't mean them then, and I certainly don't
stand by them now.

You are the best. I don't know what I'll do
when you're gone. Sometimes I cry at night
thinking about what a day without you would
be like. I can't imagine life without you.

XoXo

C

Dear Dad,

We're giving you a second chance. Please don't ruin it. We gave up everything. Don't break Mom's heart again. Don't break my heart again. We really love you, but I'm scared.

Your baby girl

Birth Mom,

Today I discovered your Instagram. It's public, my window into your world. Seeing pictures of your happy family confuses my emotions. Part of me is envious of your kids, for having you, and for having such an awesome childhood full of opportunity and happiness. You look like a pretty freaking cool mom. I mean, you have an Instagram; I don't think my mom knows what that is. I'm happy and envious of your kids' opportunity to have a childhood. I have some happy memories, and I had a great childhood, but most of my memories are tainted with yelling and tension.

I saw a picture you posted of an American Girl doll, presumably belonging to your daughter. I was momentarily emotional because I remembered being her age and longing so desperately for one, but we didn't have that kind of money to spend on a toy. I got the knockoff and was just as happy, but it's stuff like that that leaves me conflicted. I have to remind myself that 20-year-old you could not see the future, and that your view of my family only had such a broad scope.

I love my mom, and I love my brother. I just have to

work for everything I have in life. I suppose my family has made me a stronger person, given me a work ethic and humility. I know when to ask for help, and I have a very unique view of this world, one that I wouldn't have if I had the opportunities others have.

I don't know what all this means. I'm just rambling at this point. I feel like while your Instagram connects me to you, it very much disconnects me as well. Without the technology I have, I guarantee I would have attempted to make contact with you, but because I can see your life from a tiny perspective, I feel like I'm allowed to make snap judgments of your family, life, and beliefs, even though those may be very wrong.

I frequently wonder if you have Facebook, Google, or Instagram stalked me. If you do, what do you think? Do you find yourself making judgments based on the tiny details of my life I choose to make public? I wonder how accurate they are. Perhaps someday I'll grow balls and actually reach out to you.

—The Daughter You Don't Know

Dear Mom,

Despite everything you've done, I'm trying my best to forgive you and move on.

I can't make things between us better on my own, and once I get out of here, I can't promise I'll keep in touch.

I can, however, promise that I will learn from your abuse, and I swear I will create a better life for myself. I won't hold as much hatred in my heart as you do.

And I'm sorry too. You're alone. I am one of the only two people you have. I can tell you have so much pain inside of you, and that's why you hurt us. I tried to help. I did my best. But I'm afraid I'm not equipped to help you, and I'm sorry. I wish I could help. But I can't.

I'm going to be distant from now on. It's probably going to hurt you a lot. I know it hurts me. But I can't stay here much longer. I can't handle the manipulation you pull. I can't handle your impossible demands and insulting, belittling comments anymore.

I'm going to do the only thing you really taught me to do well. I'm going to work my ass off. And then I'm going to leave.

—A.K.

Big sister,

Your husband hits me.

I just thought you should know.

Little sister

Dear Brother,

I haven't had a real conversation with you in nearly 7 years. The sad thing is: we live under the same roof. I don't know what changed when you went to high school, but I miss being able to joke with my brother. All the interaction I get from you now are critical comments or you laughing at me or you making fun of me or you getting mad at me.

I hate that I don't even know what your favourite colour is. I don't know anything about you anymore, and it's terrible. All I know about your personality is what you allow us to see. I have no idea how you are with your friends, or what kind of things you like (apart from computers and such). It's all the simple things that I don't know, because I only see you a couple times a day.

I wish you would get past whatever phase you're in. I don't want to be one of those people who never talk to their sibling. *I want to know who you are.*

From,
Your sister

R,

I'm your older sister, and it hurts when you
treat me like you hate me. I think you're
being bullied, I think your friends are
assholes, and I think you deserve the
world, but you won't listen to me.

   If I could give you everything, R,
I would. But you need to make your own
mistakes, even if it hurts to watch you do
so. I'm here if, when, you need me.

Your doting sister,
G

Dear my older brother,

I understand you love me, that you care for your
little sister. I remember you beat up a bully once
on the bus, and how you kept that frightening
image of yourself for the sake of my safety.
I remember how ever since we were young and I
cried, you would go out of your way to make me
calm down. When you found out who I liked, you
would secretly interrogate their older siblings to
figure out what this guy was like.

But you don't need to worry anymore. That
was almost a decade ago. You're an adult now.
You need to live your own life. I'm not yours to
baby anymore, because soon I'll be an adult too.

Love,
Your little sister

DEAR R,
YOU WEREN'T EVEN
BRAVE ENOUGH TO
BREAK MY HEART.
YOU JUST CRUMPLED
IT BEHIND YOUR BACK.

WISH YOU
WERE STILL
MINE (IF YOU
EVER WERE),
J

Dear C,

It's a terrible feeling to love someone, knowing they don't feel the same. But it's even worse to love someone thinking you've got a chance when you don't.

I was so sure you loved me. I was so sure every time I saw you that this would be the day you would admit it. I thought it was just nerves getting in the way of us. I kept hoping, and dreaming, and filling my mind with fantasies. I finally realized I wasn't what you wanted. That broke my heart. I tried to shut you out.

I've changed now, yet in the back of my mind you're forever there. I haven't forgotten about you. If you love me, let me know. I'll be there, ready to fall into your arms. But I don't think that wish will ever come true. No matter how many dandelions I blow on and scatter into the air. No matter how many 11:11s I stare at. No matter how many eyelashes I find on my cheeks.

E

Dear J,

For the most part I have come to terms
that our relationship, our plans for the
future, and our love are over, but the
other day a thought crossed my mind.

Instead of being the wife who asks
about your past loves, I will be the person
you think of when she asks that question.

This thought haunts me now.

—B

E,
IT MAKES ME
SAD THAT THE BEST
DAYS WERE THE
ONES I GOT TO
SEE YOU, AND
NOW THE BEST
DAYS ARE THE
ONES WHERE
I DON'T.

—J

To the one who will love him next,

He gets frustrated when he gets a bad mark on a maths test. Don't do anything but sit there with him in silence, because you will only irritate him further if you try to comfort him. He's stubborn like that.

Let him share his music with you. In fact, initiate a conversation about the tunes he listens to when he isn't talking to you on the phone. I promise you won't like everything he shows you, but I do promise that humoring him is bound to make your skin heat because the smile that graces his face is worth the occasional shitty song.

Call him. Don't text him. Listening to him laugh at your poor jokes will make your week.

When he starts to complain about his mother or the man she married only months after divorcing his father, hug him even if he says he's fine. He's not fine.

Dr. Pepper is his favorite, never get him Mr. Pibb instead.

Allow him to cuddle you and spoil you, because his overactive mind takes him to places of doubt and insecurity if you don't.

Love him with everything you have, I implore you to do so. He is a free spirit that will be gone before your eyes if you allow him to, and there's nothing more destroying than realizing all you have left of him are memories and the smell of his scent on articles of your clothing. He's a force to be reckoned with. Admire him, treasure him, love him.

Sincerely,
A name you may hear in passing,
a name associated with buried memories

C

GET OUT OF MY
DREAMS. THEY'RE THE
ONLY PLACE I STILL
SEE YOU AND I
NEED TO MOVE ON.

M

My Favourite Rockstar,

You introduced me to all the music that I listen to now. I can't stand what everyone else is listening to, but everything I like reminds me of you. Each chord echoes in my head the way it did in your garage. Each drumbeat slams into my heart the way it did at your biggest gig. Each melody runs through my veins the way adrenaline coursed through my body when you touched me. Everything I hear sounds like you, but silence just sounds like me, all alone. I don't know which one makes me cry more.

—Still Your Biggest Fan

Dear S,

Let me be your friend. And only your friend. I beg you, please. When your girlfriend jokingly says, "Stop looking at him like that, like you love him," then pay heed. Let us be normal. Let us just be two boys that are friends. Let's see what that's like again. Don't let me wonder if you still think of the night we first kissed, drunk in the light of your fridge, with Bon Jovi playing in the background, or back to the nights under the stars.

   I've met your girlfriend. I've traveled a country with you and her, and I adore her as much as I love your drunken dreamy crooked gaze on me.

   You have to let me go. You have to let me let you go.

C

M,

The last time it snowed like this we spent all day inside. I made you watch *Ferris Bueller* and you kissed me goodnight and then called the second I left the room so we could talk until we fell asleep.

But then again, the last time it snowed like this you were still mine.

Give the new girl my best,
C

N

MY MEMORIES OF YOU
PLAGUE MY MIND.

IT IS BOTH TOXIC
& INTOXICATING.

I CAN'T SEEM TO MAKE
IT STOP, BUT IT HURTS
SO GOOD.

M

G,

I LOST MY
PROMISE RING.
GOOD
THING
YOU LOST YOUR
PROMISE MONTHS
AGO.

M

Dear S,

In a foreign city of a million people,
it was fate that brought us to each other.
You were my first everything. Our summer
together was a movie that I hope has not
ended yet. I like to believe that we are
simply taking a break to get the budget we
need to continue filming. I hope it's you
and me together in the end credits.

Don't forget about me.

—W

t,

ANYONE AFTER YOU WILL
KNOW WHO YOU ARE. EVEN
IF I DON'T TELL THEM YOUR
NAME. THEY'LL SEE WHERE PIECES
OF YOU USED TO FIT IN
ME AND THEY'LL SEE WHERE
I'M EMPTY AND CRAVING YOU.
THEY MIGHT NOT KNOW
YOUR FACE, BUT THEY'LL  KNOW
THAT THE BEST PARTS OF ME
WERE ALWAYS YOURS.

M

DEAR J,
I'M SORRY I DRUNK TEXTED
YOU. I'M SORRY I PUSHED
YOU AWAY. I'M SORRY I GO
HOME WITH EVERYONE
BUT YOU. I'M SORRY I
DIDN'T KNOW WHAT I
HAD WHEN I HAD THE
CHANCE. I'M NOT
SORRY FOR FALLING IN
LOVE, BUT I'M SORRY
FOR FALLING TOO LATE.
                LOVE,
                    C

DEAR K,

I KNOW the WORLD'S
not OVER. But mine SURE
as hell FEELS LIKE it. YOUR
WORDS KnockED the WIND
out of me and I DON'T
KNOW IF I'LL EVER BE ABLE
to BREATHE AGAIN. how
DO I put my PIECES BACK
togethER when you
WERE my GLUE?

C

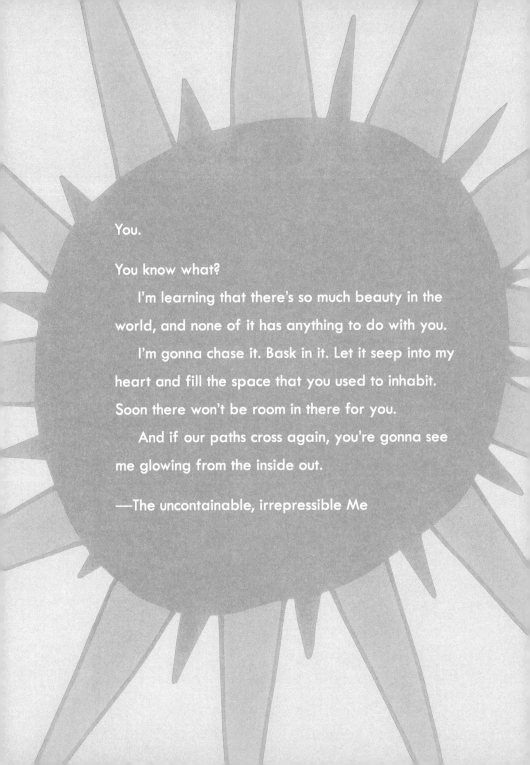

You.

You know what?

   I'm learning that there's so much beauty in the world, and none of it has anything to do with you.

   I'm gonna chase it. Bask in it. Let it seep into my heart and fill the space that you used to inhabit. Soon there won't be room in there for you.

   And if our paths cross again, you're gonna see me glowing from the inside out.

   —The uncontainable, irrepressible Me

Dear O,

Okay. I miss you. I miss you in a small, constant ache.

When I met you, I collected you. I picked up your little mannerisms and put them together to form a carbon copy of you inside my brain to seemingly keep forever. I learned the way you talked, how you ate two sandwiches for lunch, how you liked chemistry and loved screenplay.

I never really learned how or why you loved me, though. I could never trust the way you said it, only how you punched little fists in your pockets and rolled around on the balls of your feet, not looking up, when I said that I could not let myself love you back.

But, as you knew, I did love you. You knew because you collected me, too. But now, we are slowly and quickly losing each other.

—A

Dear N,

Please choose me over the alcohol.
Please. I'm tired of watching you
waste away because you're so scared.
I want to grow old together. This
isn't what you promised.

Sincerely,
Your dearly devoted K

K

Maybe one day when we're older and wiser, our paths will cross again and we can do it right. You're the love of my life. I can't believe I let that slip away. I hope one day it'll come back.

All of my love and apologies are forever yours, as am I.

S

Dear E,

I used to think that you're supposed to go through pain for someone you're in love with, as if it were romantic, and proof of the extent of your love for them.

It turns out that the pain you put me through wasn't love. It was just vulnerability that you exploited.

You let me down.

—P

Dear Casey,

Oftentimes heartache is associated with midnight, romanticizing the idea that the loss is unbearable enough to keep you awake at night. But loss is not solemnly accompanied by insomnia.

Because it's 11:50 a.m. and I'm sitting in the back of my history class unable to cope with the lesson, let alone write it down, because all my thoughts stink of you and scream out your name in aching need to be bled onto paper.

Because my fingers are frostbitten and all I can think about is the air of New York, and if this is how it feels for you when you leave the warmth of your home and venture into the cold January air.

Because it's 12:00 p.m. and my day is drenched in you.

Because you're nowhere and everywhere.

Because I can sleep, but I'd rather not because I hate dreaming of you, and waking up to the reality that you're not here.

Because it's 12:05 p.m., and I miss you.

Love,
L

S

we always used
to listen to sad
songs together.
i never thought
that we would
become our
own sad song.
m

Dear I,

When I told you that I'd always love you, I wasn't saying it just to be cute. I was saying it because I meant it. Even now, seven months after you left, six months after you told me you didn't love me anymore, five months after you started dating her, and one month after I started dating him, I still love you. Because my love was real.

Sincerely,
D

Dear J,

Your surname is Hope.
I guess it's ironic
that my hope left
when you did.

Love,
E

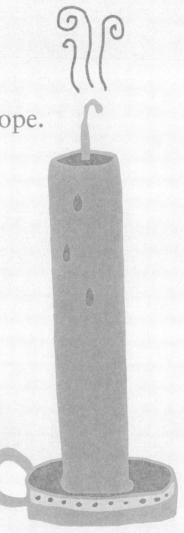

D,

YOU WERE THE
PERSON WHO
HELPED ME FIND
MY CURRENT THERAPIST,
AND NOW YOU'RE
THE REASON I'M
GOING TO THERAPY.

P

Dear the one who doesn't care,

You left your watch at my place and the ticking keeps me up at night because it reminds me of your beating heart. In the morning when you were gone I could still feel you on my sheets. You were all over me and I tried to wash you off of my skin, but somehow you're still here and it hurts so much that sometimes I hold my breath not to feel you. Maybe you crawled into my veins and that's why I don't know how to be myself anymore.

Someone who wanted to be your everything but was your nothing,
N

S,

I WANT MY
FIRST KISS
BACK.

C

TDC –

I just pretend
you never
happened.

—R

D,

I'm sorry.

I'm sorry I had to move on so fast;
he's not even right for me. But I need to
get you off my mind and this is the only
way I know how. I'm sorry to him too.
He deserves all that I cannot give. I gave
it all to you.

It's been a little over a month.
I pushed all your stuff away; the giant
gorilla is my sister's now. Your key chain
won't leave my keys, though.

—A

Dear L—

You once told me that if I were a
feeling,
  I'd be the feeling you get
when walking into a warm room
from out in the cold.
  I'd give anything to feel that
way again.

J

UNREQUItED LOVE

P,

it's HARD

falling so hard

FOR SOMEONE

WHO BARELY

TRIPPED.

N

dear s,

this is so shitty of me to say or do but i just literally think about you every day. ever since we got closer this year i just argh. i really truly deeply love you. you are so much to me. i think of you when i buy shampoo, when i brush my teeth, when i make my bed. every word in every book. stop being so effortlessly lovely. i wish you felt the same as i do.

all of my world,

c

Dear I,

Please look at me the way you look at Andromeda. If you came down from space once in a while, you would see that I can be just as good as a hundred constellations.

P

DEAREST J,

IT SEEMS LIKE
YOU'VE FOUND
A SHINING STAR
TO LIGHT YOUR
NIGHT SKY.

I WISH I WAS
HER.

D

Dear N,

Almost three years later you would never think that I still love you just as much as I did the first time you held my hand.

You crushed me into a million tiny pieces, which wouldn't have been so bad if you didn't pick them back up and place them in my hand and tell me I'm on my own now.

You were my best friend, my everything, you were my first love. I'm so very glad we can still talk sometimes, even though it kills me when the conversation ends. I miss you more than words can explain.

I dream and think about you every day. I only wish you would realize. Everyone yells at me for being stuck on you for so long, but they just don't get it.

I know you think about me too. I know you talk about me sometimes. Your friends aren't as good at keeping secrets as you think they are.

Always waiting,

D

B,

PART OF ME
THINKS I CAN'T
STOP LOVING
YOU. BUT THE OTHER
PART KNOWS
I CAN'T KEEP
WAITING.

—A

CX,

I think WE WERE both in love at different points —
and I wish more than anything fate had pulled us together at the right moment.

A

Dear C,

I'm sorry it took me six years, four
rejections, three boyfriends, and countless
efforts to realize I love you. I have fallen
head over heels for you, but I know it's
too late now. I don't deserve to be loved
by someone so special after I broke your
heart, but please give me a chance to make
things right.

M

V,

YOU WILL ALWAYS
BE MY FAVORITE
WHAT-IF.

/          T

Dear S,

I guess it's too late now. You're off doing what you always told me you've dreamed of doing, and I'm here doing what my parents have always dreamed I'd end up doing. I guess being childhood friends doesn't guarantee staying together.

I regret not telling you that I loved you.

But I'm not writing this to have my feelings returned. No, I'm writing this to let you know that I'll probably never tell you. I'm writing this because I know I'll never get the courage, let alone the chance, to tell you because you're so far away now.

Hey, on the off chance that telepathy works or that you have powers to know everything, I want you to know that I love you—not just as a childhood friend, but as someone I want to marry.

J

A

I lost my virginity to someone I just
met because he reminded me of you.
   You never liked me in that way,
and now you're seeing someone else.
It hurts. I could sleep with him again,
and I might, but I know it'll only make
me feel worse.

L

DEAR G,
I'VE FALLEN FOR
YOU, BUT YOU'VE
FALLEN FOR HER.

—S

Dear trans boy from high school,

There's so much that I could never tell you. There's so much that I still want to know about you.

Every time I go downtown, I secretly hope to see you. I hope that you'll notice me as well and that we'll hang on just to chat.

I hope that you'll notice how much I've changed, how different I look, because I really want you to know that I've realized I'm trans as well. I don't know why, but I want you to know that you weren't the only one. I want you to see this side of me. I want you to be proud of me.

I used to have a crush on you and I guess I still have. It's just that we don't see each other anymore, so there isn't really much to crush about. It's like my feelings for you are paused or frozen, but I'm sure

I would develop feelings again if we ever got into contact again.

I wonder how you've been. I miss you more than you can imagine.

I used to look up to you, you know? Maybe I just had a crush on you because I wanted to be like you. You were out and about and so confident about your gender. No one said mean things about you behind your back or at least I didn't ever witness it. Everyone was so accepting. Even the teachers. You were so nice and kind and amazing and the boys still accepted you as one of them. I wanted to be just like you.

If our graduating class ever hosted a class reunion, I think I would attend just to see you. Would you go as well?

M

To the ever-lovely H,

I didn't know what unrequited love was until I met
your best friend. But he was the poster boy for
unavailable, and you were around, and actually
seemed to like me. I'd never known that could
happen. So I settled, and I guess now I'm using
you to catch glimpses of him every now and again.

I'm sorry I don't love you. But I love him,
and you're my only way forward.

Does it make me a shitty person if I don't
feel too bad about that?

Not yours,
R xxx

JD,

I am going to
make you wish
you'd chosen
me.

—CND

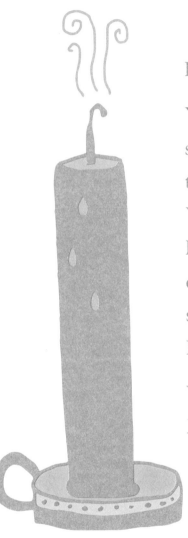

L,

Yesterday I told you I couldn't see myself taking part in the traditionally terrifying forever. You smiled and told me when I find the one it would be different. It would have been so easy to tell you then. But I didn't.

With love,

M

K—
IF ONLY
YOU

WEREN'T
STRAIGHT.
—S

A,

It scares me sometimes, how much my happiness relies on you. It scares me because I know there will be a time when you aren't near me, and I don't know what I'm going to do then.

You have no idea, though, how much you mean to me. I long to tell you and the words "I love you" always seem to be on the tip of my tongue, but I do not want to lose out on being your friend by spilling my feelings unnecessarily.

So in case you think all of those poems were about you and this letter is addressed to you, you are 100 percent right. But you probably don't and may never find this. And that's the point.

Sending all of my love your way,
E

J,
i think you're
my soul mate.
but I don't think
I'm yours.
have you ever
heard of something
more sad?
-A

Dear Emily,

You've taken my breath away. I don't ever want it back. You've stolen my heart. How about you give me yours for safekeeping? I'm surrounded by your warm personality and beautiful face. You are my everything . . . but I am your nothing.

—R

Dear D,

I DID CHEat on you with Him. I LOVE you and you're the most PERFECt man any woman COULD ask FOR — But you're not Him.

I'm SORRY.

L

**The Person Who Didn't Care Enough,**

I don't know what I was expecting.

Maybe I was expecting you to **apologize.**

Maybe I didn't think you would see me crying and **laugh.**

Maybe I thought you would ask me to **stay.**

Maybe I wanted you to tell me you loved me and didn't want to give up on **us.**

Maybe I hoped you would finally **change.**

I wasn't expecting you to walk away.

**—The Person Who Cared Too Much**

Ben—

I've written you so many letters, some on here, some in that purple book I keep by my bedside, and every time I ask myself why I haven't told you everything I've written down. I know I'll never send them, and you'll never see them, but god, there's this irrational part of me that wants you to.

I've been in love with you for three years, and I know you feel the same because you've told me so, but the timing's never been right. We've had so many missed opportunities and now, when the timing's worse than it's ever been, now we finally make a move on each other. I hate what I've become because I can't control how I feel about you or the way my body reacts when your hands are on my skin.

*Cheater.*

That's what we're doing. Every time you're with me, you're cheating on her. It's not fair, to her, to me, to you, but every time we tell ourselves that we're gonna stop, that we're gonna reinstate the boundaries that have never really existed with us, it happens again, and we both feel even guiltier than before.

You can't keep telling me that there's "something there between us" or that "things could change" because god, it hurts! You can't keep dangling it over my head like a prize to be won because I don't want to wait for you. I can't function without you in my life, but I can't wait for you to make up your mind. I can't keep breaking my heart and hers because you can't decide how you feel.

I love you, but I don't think I can be in love with you anymore.

And I think that hurts more than anything else.

—S

TO S,

I KISSED

HIM

FIRST.

—B

Dear R,

A few months ago, I had to make a choice. I didn't think I was the sort of boy who would even have one girl interested, let alone two at the same time. And I chose her. And I chose wrong.

This seems almost too ridiculous to write, but you were too perfect. We were too similar. I thought it was too good to be true. I thought something so incredible could never happen to me.

I didn't go with you because I thought that if it went badly, it would be devastating. But that's nothing compared to the realization that I was so spectacularly, irreversibly wrong.

Yours, A

Dear SC,

I just wanted to let you know that we'll
never be together again, we're done.
You won't use me again. I don't miss you.
I'm so much happier and better off
without you.

  Have a great life, I hope you're
happy.

Formerly yours,
AB

Boyfriend,

We have been together for three years, but I'm falling for someone else. I love you more than I can comprehend, and when he isn't around, I feel zero doubt.

Whenever he is there, I can't help but look at him, notice him. There's some sort of animal magnetism that drives me nuts. I've dreamt of him for two weeks, all while sleeping next to you.

The very worst part is, he is your best friend. I hate myself more than anything for letting this happen. I don't know if he feels anything for me, but if he were to try something I don't know if I could control myself.

Sometimes I wonder if I should let you go and never see either of you again so I don't ruin you like I've ruined others before.

I'm a monster. I love you so much but I don't know how much longer I can keep myself together.

Please move to the East Coast like you said you might, so we can blame things on the distance and not on me being an absolutely terrible person.

Love,

S

Dear boy with a girlfriend,

Last night you held me for hours and it was the safest I have ever felt in my life. You ran your fingers through my hair and pulled me close and I was so happy I wanted to explode.

This morning you woke up and said you didn't remember anything from last night even though you were completely sober. And then you told my friends that I was all over you and that you tried to stop me.

Just because you feel guilty about it doesn't mean you can blame your choices on other people. It kills me to know that what seems like a huge mistake to you was actually one of the happiest moments of my life.

Sincerely,
The person who has loved you for three years

Dear J,

You're holding me hostage. You were the first person I opened up to about being gay, but you're the last person I want to know.

—P

A,

It's been five years since we took that picture in the
bowling alley. The first time I saw your smile it felt like
it was made just for me. Now, when I see it, I want to
wipe it right off of your face.

Our relationship wasn't lengthy or tragic or anything
particularly interesting. You were my first since that
terrible thing that happened to me when I was only a
child. You were one of the first people I ever told about
what happened to me. You cried in my arms.

Then, fast-forward about a year and a half. We're
at a party, haven't spoken in nearly nine months, and I
push my limits. I drink a little and get a little loud. You
drink and sit in the corner, brooding and staring.

I find a place to rest my head for the night, and
you come in—uninvited. You lie with me. I push you
away. You can't comprehend the word no. I'm too
drunk to remember until months later when you confess

what happened. You didn't lose control entirely, but enough to make me hate you.

You were my first love, and you betrayed me in the worst way possible. You brought me back to that place of weakness from when I was young.

And you had the guts to think we could be friends? We will never, ever be friends. You can't disregard someone as a human being and then expect me to care about you.

You cannot violate my trust and my boundaries and expect me to forget.

Now, when I see you around, I won't say a word. You don't deserve even that. I have forgiven you. Not for your sake. For mine. Your burdens are not mine to carry. Your life is not mine to worry about.

It's been five years since we took that picture and I finally have the courage to throw it away.

—S

Dear R,

I just hurt someone
like you hurt me.

You're starting
to seem a bit
more human.

J

W,

You should get an Academy
Award for stringing me
along for so long.
   I was young and stupid. If
I could, I would go back and
break up with you the first
time you cheated on me.

E

dear tigger—

I'm sorry. I'm so sorry for
everything I put you through
and everything I've said to you
and every single bruise I've left
on your heart.

I'm sorry for wasting your time
and trying to hold on to you
even though I gave you up. I'm
sorry for being upset when I made
you think I was still yours.

I love you so deeply and so dearly
but I'm afraid if we continue
things the way they are going,
I'll end up hating you. I don't want
to. you've been too good to me.
please stop loving me. I don't
deserve it.

　　　　　　　　　—pooh

L,

We found the ring in your desk. I would have said yes.

A

Dear Ty,

It kills me that I never got to say
goodbye. I'm sorry, I didn't know
that would be the last time I saw
you. I would have said something
more than just "Bye."

—Sarah

G,

HE'S THREE MONTHS OLD AND I WISH
YOU WERE HERE TO SEE HIM GROW. HE
LOOKS SO MUCH LIKE YOU, BIG DARK
EYES AND A CHEEKY GRIN. HE'S STARTED
LAUGHING, GIGGLING TO HIMSELF.
YOUR BROTHER CAN MAKE HIM LAUGH
LIKE NO OTHER.

YOUR MOTHER CAN'T GET OVER HOW
MUCH HE LOOKS LIKE YOU. I THINK
IT GETS HER THROUGH THE DARK DAYS
WHERE IT REALLY HITS HER HARD THAT
SHE'S LOST HER ELDEST SON.

I WISH YOU'D KNOWN ABOUT HIM
BEFORE YOU MADE THE DECISION
TO END YOUR LIFE. I WISH I'D KNOWN
A FEW DAYS EARLIER AND MAYBE

THAT WOULD HAVE STOPPED YOU.
I TALK ABOUT YOU ALL THE TIME.
HE WILL ALWAYS KNOW HOW MUCH
STRENGTH HIS DAD HAD AND HOW
BRAVE HE WAS.

SOMETIMES I STRUGGLE. SOMETIMES
I NEED YOU HERE. HE NEEDS YOU
HERE. SOMETIMES I JUST WANT
SOMEONE TO TELL ME I'M DOING
AN OKAY JOB IN BRINGING HIM UP
ALONE, OUR SON, WITHOUT YOU.

SOMETIMES I JUST WANT SOMEBODY
TO TELL ME THAT IT'S OKAY TO
FEEL LIKE THIS.

LOVE YOU ALWAYS,

E

Dear W,

It has been almost two years. Two years since we were scared teenagers who made the hardest decision of our lives. I don't blame you for asking me to get the abortion, because I know it was best for us. I just wish you had helped me pick up the pieces afterwards. I know it still haunts you like it does me. I know that's why we don't talk anymore. It hurts too much. But I truly hope one day we will find some closure together. You are such a great guy, and you deserve happiness.

Love,
M

Dear S,

I wish I'd talked to you on your last night here. I wish I'd told you how much I love you and what you mean to me as my sister. I don't know if I could have changed your mind; I'd like to think that you'd still be here with me.

Now, nearly four years later, I'm left with unbearable regret and helplessness at my inability to help you. I'm your older sister, isn't that what I'm supposed to do? Now you're gone, and I can't change that.

I just hope that you're resting peacefully now, and that you know how much you are loved and missed.

Love always,
P

P.S. Reader: If you're depressed and wishing your life would end, don't follow in my sister's footsteps. Suicide is an awful thing and it leaves a lasting impact on the ones that get left behind.

DEAR SALLY,
YOU'RE NOT HERE ANYMORE,
AND I DON'T WANT TO BE HERE
ANYMORE EITHER. BUT I KNOW
IF I'M GONE NOBODY WILL
WATER THE FLOWERS I
PLANTED NEXT TO YOUR
GRAVE. THIS ALL FEELS LIKE
MY FAULT SOMEHOW AND
I MISS YOU SO MUCH IT
HURTS.

ALL MY LOVE,
H

K,

You died 15 months ago today, but contrary to what everyone keeps telling me, time does not heal all wounds. I still miss you just as much as I did the moment I found out. I know you will never see this, but since it hurts too much to say it out loud I'll just say it here— I love you. I will always love you. I've tried to stay strong for C's sake, but I think she knows I'm starting to crumble. I don't know how much longer I can keep up this brave face. You were the best cousin in the entire world; you were practically my older brother. This world isn't the same without you. My deepest regret is never being able to say a proper goodbye to you. I miss you more than I can put into words.

All my love,
S

G,

It's been one year, one year exactly, since the day you made your last decision.

I've never once stopped thinking about you, or the times we spent together. The times we would lie, just lie, in your bed. We wouldn't talk, but no words needed to be said, did they?

The stupid arguments we had, and then the making-up. People thought we weren't right and we didn't work, the arguments were too much. But that was just us, you would say. Who wants to be normal?

I remember that day vividly, the petty argument we had over you not answering your phone. You stormed out, but that was normal. You left, but not before telling me that you love me. I didn't reply. That was how we were. God, how I wish I replied. How I wish I could go back and run after you and tell you how much I love you and I need you in my life. How your little brother can't cope without you. How we all would have helped.

I remember you not coming home that night, but then again, that was normal. I remember your brother telling me that they'd found you, in our spot in the woods, and giving me the piece of paper you had. The last thing you ever wrote, telling me that I was too good for you and you will forever love me.

It's been a year, a year today exactly, and I still can't come to terms with it. You made that decision, to leave us all behind and to end your suffering. There's been no one else, and quite frankly I can never see there being anyone else.

It's been a year, but it still hurts like it was yesterday.

I'm sitting in our spot writing this, leaning up against the big oak tree, the exact location where you made your decision to silence your demons and end your suffering.

I miss you just isn't enough.

Forever in love with you,
Your E

C,

I Don't KNOW WHY
I DIDn't CALL YOU,
BUt It IS MY BIGGESt
REGREt. I'LL NEVER
FORGIVE MYSELF.
I COULDN'T HAVE
SAVED YOU, I KNOW
tHAt NOW.
BUt tHAT DOESN't MAKE
It HURt ANY LESS.

E

Dear Mama,

Whenever I would come home, no matter how long it had been, you would react the same way: the second you heard my voice you would smile. You would stand up at my urging and give me a hug, and sometimes, if I asked for it, a kiss on the cheek. You would look at me with such love that I would sometimes feel embarrassed, and you wouldn't stop smiling until I left. Even though I lost you in some ways when you fell ill, I knew that you were still my mother and you still loved me just as much. It didn't matter if I didn't have any friends, if I dropped out of school, if the rest of the family was angry with me, if I was a failure: I had you. You were my only physical example of unconditional love, and with you, I was Superwoman.

I struggle on without you, but I will never allow my heart to be severed from yours. I love you forever, Mama. Four months down, a lifetime to go.

Pray for me.

All my love,
Your lonely daughter

Dear Sally,

I'm so sorry. Everyone keeps telling me
it isn't my fault but it feels like after all
those times I sat up all night to make sure
you were still breathing I really let you
down this time. I couldn't sit vigil anymore.
All I have left is your bandanna and a
patch of wildflowers that won't bloom.
Seeing you die has given me nightmares
and so much guilt I don't know what to
do with it. I'm not religious but given any
theory about a God or afterlife is true,
then you're somewhere pleasant like you
deserve. Sally, you never got what you
deserved and I am so sorry. I love you.

HM

Dear My Dog,

I look for you before I put my feet down
off the couch. I snap my fingers for you
to make sure I don't shut you in the dark
accidentally. I call your name to come clean
up my kitchen mess. I expect you at my heel.
I turn to catch you out of the corner of my
eye. Shadows trick me with you. You aren't
there and my memories are
leaking down my face.
I held you as you fell
asleep. Walking away
from your still form was
the hardest thing I've
done. I miss you so much,
and your belly smelling
of popcorn. Love me and
forgive me.

Your Person

Dear H, my dearest H,

My heart aches when I think of you. These past 12 days
have been truly horrible, I've been lacking sleep, because
I can't stop myself from seeing you, lying there in that
bush, exposed to the world, lifeless, even if it's just an
image I came up with. I haven't seen you in 16 days and
I will never see you again, even though I visit you every
day. It feels wrong, everything here feels wrong. People
lit candles for you. I did. Every day since it happened,
since you left, since that day that changed me in some
way. It's hard, you know? We meet up now every evening
and sit there together, but it's no longer you, D, H and
me, it's not our usual circle anymore. It's just us three and
random other people and it feels wrong not to see you
scrunching up your little nose and pulling your head back
a little, asking us what we were thinking while doing
random things. I will never feel your weird little fingers
pinching my arm again because you have to contain your
laughter. We will never tease anyone again together or
just prank someone. I will never hear you talk about your
favourite lipstick again or this new bag you bought that
you'd grown to love dearly. I will never see you roll your

eyes again at the stupid things I do and you will never tell me again that my music taste is shit.

I never thought I could cry so much in such a little time. You'd probably want me to laugh again, like you always did, and I can laugh when I remember the stupid things we did together.

I know you hated romantics, but I love you and I always will. I will always carry you in my heart; no matter where I go or how often I think of you, you'll still be there.

We had so many plans together, and they were stolen from us in the most horrible way possible. I don't know how anyone could ever do this to you.

I hope you're happy now, and in a better place, and I hope you keep an eye on your sister and family in general. I hope you keep an eye on us as well, on all of your friends. And I hope you're wearing that outfit now, the one you told me about. And I hope you're eating lasagna, like we planned to do together. I hope you fulfill all your dreams now. I know you can.

In undying love,
E

DEAR L,

YOU SHOULD HAVE tOLD ME YOU
WEREN't GOING to MAKE It
tHROUGH CHRIStMAS. I HAVE

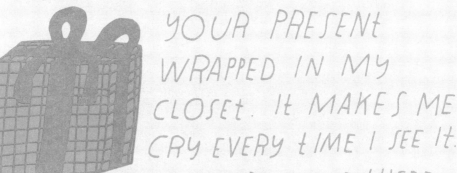

YOUR PRESENt
WRAPPED IN MY
CLOSEt. It MAKES ME
CRY EVERY tIME I SEE It.

IF YOU SEE tHIS FROM UP tHERE,
tHEN PLEASE KNOW I LOVE YOU
AND I WAS GOING tO GEt YOU
tHAt SHIRt YOU HAD YOUR
EYE ON.                    LOVE,
                              G

G,

You called me during your two free minutes waiting for your brother in the parking lot, and it left me **smiling** for the next half hour. Thank you for making even small conversations seem like the most **wonderful things in the world.**

Yours,

T

Dear J,

Sometimes I squeeze your hand three times when I hold it, and you squeeze back. What you don't know is it means "I love you," and those words are not something you're ready to hear.

Someday, I'll tell you. But for now, I'm happy just loving you in silence.

Thank you for being in my life.

—A

To my exes,

Thank you. No, seriously, thank you. Because of the things we've gone through, the experiences we shared, the different lifestyles I've come across, I'm now a more mature, open-minded, and grateful person. Every single one of you has taught me a valuable lesson on life, and how to deal/cope with things. Y'all have left a piece of you in me that reminds me of what to do and what not to do. You taught me that I do need to love myself before I can give love out. You taught me that nothing is perfect. You taught me not to open myself up so easily. 'Cause of you, I think things more thoroughly. No, I may not have found "the one," but I do know that if I go looking for her, I'll never find her. So y'all have taught me the value of patience. That's the patience to do my own thing, and let her come to me when the time is right. So, again, thank you for all the experiences, and the lifelong lessons that I'll forever keep.

Sincerely,
Broken, but stronger than ever

A,

Thank you for teaching me that you don't have to be dating someone for them to break your heart. Thank you for being such an asshole that it has shown me that I have some really wonderful people around me who care a lot more than you.

M

Dear Ex-Boyfriend,

I really loved you and wanted to marry you. When you broke up with me I was crushed. Looking back, I appreciate that you did. Thank you, because you did me a favor. You're a horrible person. Love truly is blind.

—S

P.S. I'm much smarter now, so thanks for that as well.

Dear J,

The five years I wasted with you turned out to be worth it. Losing you meant I found myself. I used to live my life to please you but now I know what it takes to make myself happy. So, thank you.

Love,
D

C—

You didn't even break my heart. You completely **shattered** it and left behind nothing but the **broken shell** of a person. You were my absolute everything and I loved you so damn much.

But now I can finally look at you and not feel the butterflies in my stomach or the pain in my chest. I can finally say **"I'm happy"** and mean it. Thank you for showing me how strong I really am. :)

—M

DEAR I,
THANK YOU FOR
BREAKING UP WITH
ME. I LEARNED TO LOVE
MYSELF IN THE
END.            —S

P.S. I NO LONGER
LOOK FOR YOUR FACE
IN CROWDED
PLACES.

To my favorite teacher, Mr. R,

So many people forget that a teacher is, at the end of the day, just another person with a life to live. You are one of the youngest teachers I have had, but somehow you just understood me better than any with their venerable stories and lessons. I was 13 when I was in your English class, but the memory of you will probably last me a lifetime.

I firstly want to thank you for making me who I am today: a writer. I always loved writing, but growing up in a Korean family was hard. English was not my first language, and I was pushed into mathematics and sciences more than I ever was towards literature. Writing was a hobby that I lost by the time I got to eighth grade, and you reopened it for me. Thanks to you, I was able to test my limits and I've even won national and international competitions. Again, this is only possible because of your influence in my life.

I also want to thank you for being a father figure to me. I don't really have one at home; we fight too much and I admit I've been hit and had objects thrown at me. I was morbidly afraid of most males growing up, and only recently was able to accept more of them as friends and peers into my life. You helped a huge part; in class if I was too quiet or unconfident in my work, you would never fail to make time to talk to me. You aren't a talker yourself, but you became one for me and I thank you so much for that. Even when my first boyfriend and I dated in the end of the school year, you would tell him to take good care of me and to not let me get hurt.

You also helped me. You knew I was struggling with my life. I was depressed, anxious, emotionally unstable. When I mentioned my want for a better high school, you helped me search for high schools to apply to. When I didn't get into my dream one and missed a day of class, you emailed me telling me that it was okay. When I was too tired to deal with other people, you let me stay in your classroom to just read or write quietly. You nurtured a seed of compassion for me to spread as I help others around me today, and I'm so thankful for this. I almost doubt I would be alive today if I were to not have met you.

Thank you most of all for just being there. It was rewarding to have graduated and to see you clapping in the front row of teachers with your suit on while I got my instrumental award and diploma. It was worth sticking it out every time I would hear the words "I am very proud of you" from you. Thank you.

From your favorite student, the quiet Kangaroo

Dear K,

One day I'll write a long letter telling you
things I've never told you in these six years,
but for now I just wanted to say thank you.
    You don't know it (and I'll probably
never tell you), but you talking to me today
got me through an anxiety attack. After J
invited me to her wedding and I freaked
out because everyone has their life together
and I don't, you talking nonsense about
how you're applying for Irish citizenship
really helped.
    So yeah, that's all for now. Thank you!

Always yours,
C

Dear R,

After B left, I was heartbroken. He took too much from me and cut me out of his life as if I was dispensable. I had lost hope. I felt lonely and not worthy of love, always a rebound. I didn't want to get close to any guy because I was completely afraid. However, you came out of the blue. . . . I didn't even like you at first, and I was about to delete your message. I'm glad I didn't and I got to know you better. You make me smile always, and you're funny and smart, and I'm glad we can share many things and I can open up. I don't know when it happened. It was gradual. Thank you for bringing me happiness.

M

# SUBMIT YOUR LETTERS

Now that you've read this collection of letters, I hope they have inspired you to write and submit your own anonymous letter. It is surprisingly cathartic, and you will be part of an ever-growing online community of support. Here's what you need to know to submit your letter.

## HOW DO I SUBMIT A LETTER?

You can use the submissions page: dearmyblank.tumblr.com/submit.
Or you can email it to dearmyblank@gmail.com.

## IS IT ANONYMOUS?

Yes. I post all letters anonymously.

## CAN I SEND IN A PICTURE OF A HANDWRITTEN LETTER?

Yes. You can do that by going to the submit page, and then changing the submission type to photo, or by emailing it in.

## IS PROFANITY ALLOWED ON THE TUMBLR?
Yes.

## DO YOU POST EVERY SUBMISSION?
I try my best to, but with thousands of submissions,
it will take a while to post some. I am just one person!

## CAN I SUBMIT SOMETHING IN A LANGUAGE
## OTHER THAN ENGLISH?
Yes—submissions in your native language are completely fine.

I look forward to hearing from you.

# ACKNOWLEDGMENTS

Dear everyone I'm thankful for,

First and foremost, I'm grateful for everyone who has submitted, shared, or read an unsent letter on Dear My Blank. None of this would be possible at all without the people who have joined our online community, and I'm forever indebted to them.

Second, I would like to thank some amazing people who have supported *Dear My Blank*, and me:

My agent, Heather Flaherty, and the team at the Bent Agency.

Thank you to Random House, especially my editor, Emily Easton, and everyone else involved in the publishing process.

Thank you to Rian, Misty, and Andy.

Thank you to Dad, Mom, Katie, Ashley, Courtney, Ethan, Rachel, Uncle Scott and Aunt Gina, Uncle Chris and Aunt Xiao Li, and the rest of my family.

You have my eternal gratitude.
Emily Trunko

## ABOUT THE AUTHOR

**EMILY TRUNKO** is an astonishing sixteen-year-old girl from the small town of Copley, Ohio. At age eleven, she started a book review blog called *On Emily's Bookshelf*, and at age fourteen she started the Clover Chain Project, dedicated to pairing up teens struggling with similar issues, which attracted local media attention. Dear My Blank was born out of Emily's personal notebook of letters that she never intended to send, and has now become an Internet sensation. Visit her Tumblrs at dearmyblank.tumblr.com and thelastmessagereceived.tumblr.com.

## ABOUT THE ILLUSTRATOR

**LISA CONGDON** is a fine artist and illustrator best known for her colorful paintings, intricate line drawings, pattern designs, and hand-lettering. She has illustrated over fifteen books, including the bestseller *Whatever You Are, Be a Good One*. She lives and works in Portland, Oregon. See more of her work at lisacongdon.com.

# THE LAST MESSAGE RECEIVED

A NOT-TO-BE-MISSED ADAPTATION
OF THE TUMBLR PHENOMENON

COMING SOON!